Kindness Is Every Step

Photos and Poems

Dwayne Cole

No act of kindness, no matter how small, is ever wasted.
— Aesop

Three things in human life are important: the first is to be kind.
The second is to be kind. And the third is to be kind.
— Henry James

The snowshoe hare shown on the front cover
visits my yard often.

He is rapidly putting on his white fur coat
as winter snows are coming soon.

I placed the rock in my yard in a way
that it would collect warm sun rays.

My furry friend loves to sit on the warm rock
when temperatures drop.

I don't know how to define kindness,
but this feels like a step in the right direction.

Dedication

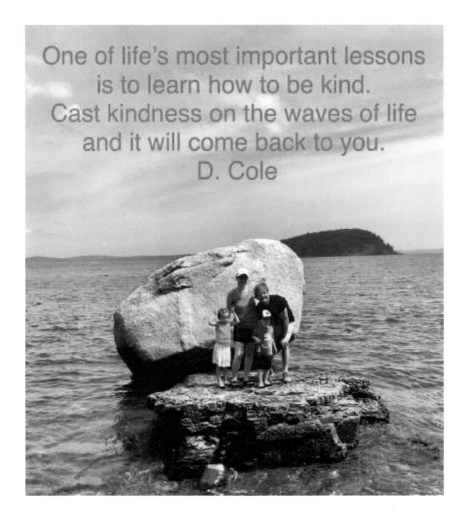

One of life's most important lessons
is to learn how to be kind.
Cast kindness on the waves of life
and it will come back to you.
D. Cole

This book is lovingly dedicated to our son, Dr. Kevin Dwayne Cole, our daughter-in-law, Susan, and our grandchildren, Anna and Matthew.

Kindness Is Every Step

**Poetry of kindness
washes from the soul
the travel stains of life**

Dwayne Cole

Parson's Porch Books

Kindness Is Every Step

ISBN: Softcover 978-1-951472-93-1

Copyright © 2021 by Dwayne Cole

Parson's Porch Books is an imprint of Parson's Porch *&* Company (PP*&*C) in Cleveland, Tennessee. PP*&*C is an innovative organization which raises money by publishing books of noted authors, representing all genres. Its face and voice is **David Russell Tullock** (dtullock@parsonsporch.com).

Parson's Porch *&* Company *turns books into bread & milk* by sharing its profits with the poor.

www.parsonsporch.com

Contents

Conclusion

Words of Kindness Acts of love
Gifts of happiness
Sweet as Heaven above

Preface

Kindness Is Every Step seeks to make a contribution to world transformation. This transformation must start with the individual, if it is to become the basis of world peace. kindness is reciprocal and moves from the individual, to the family, and to the world family. When this innate psychological need of relatedness is met, we are productive and happy. In this relational and all-inclusive sense—

Kindness Is Everything

There is an organic affinity
between kindness and happiness.

If you want to be happy.
Be kind to yourself.

If you want others to be happy.
Be kind to them.

If you want nature to be happy.
Be kind to birds, flowers, bees, and trees.

If you want the world to be happy

Be kind.

These poems are a journey in this direction. By mindfully practicing kindness transformation occurs at all levels of society. Kindness is in every step and leads to peace, a harmony of harmonies.

Introduction

"If we had taken up this habit of kindness long ago,
before we fell into darkness,
what suffering might we have spared the world
and ourselves?" (Olivia Hawker's, *The Ragged Edge of Night*,
p.72. Set in a small village in Nazi Germany during WW II).

Kindness is an undeniable human experience
seen in most organized societies and religions.
In the Bible kindness is grounded in God,
and kindness may appropriately be designated as God.
In Exodus 33:19, God's self-designation is,
"I am merciful and kind."

God uniquely shares kindness out of fullness,
giving all entities aim and purpose.
Where kindness reigns every day is a dream
and every tomorrow a vision of hope.
Kindness is poetry from unseen realms.
God is the poem. God is kind.

As used in the biblical covenant
between God and God's people,
grace always implies a gracious turning of God
in kindness to heal brokenness
and restore covenant relationships.

In the Greek New Testament, χαρις, the word for grace,
is found about 175 times—
In 24 of the 27 books of the Greek New Testament.
Tracing the word from its first use in classical Greek
reveals that this Greek word, *karis*, is best translated as kindness,
though often translated as grace.

The Gospels and Epistles of the New Testament
begin and end with gracious kindness.
Kindness in these writings of the early Church
is the fruit of Jesus' gentle life and tender teachings,

wrapped in the compassionate words from the cross,
"Father, forgive them."

This book, *Kindness Is Every Step,*
is a call for—
A Revolution of Kindness.

My loving parents taught me
that kindness is hidden
in every word and deed.

The Bible reveals God's kindness
in the prophets and Psalmists
of the Old Testament;

and in Jesus' gentle life
and tender teachings
empowered by God's Spirit
in the New Testament.

In my ministry of 50 years
I experienced the transforming power
of kind words and actions.

In retirement, my contemplative lifestyle in Alaska
reveals that kindness is hiding
in the world of nature around us,
and may be designated as an evolutionary principle.

Nature is unselfishly kind—
Shares with one and all
without distinction.

Let us learn to love the earth
by celebrating it openly
rather than by possessing it.

Instead of building walls
Let us build bridges to span
our differences.

A kindness revolution calls
for courageous action of all faiths—
Millions of quiet transformations.

We are in a suffering wounded world,
with walking caravans of refugees
who have not been treated kindly.
They are seeking justice, a kind haven.

A kind world of justice
is struggling to be born.
Be kind to one another.
        (Ephesians 4:32)

Please do not dismiss these poems
as the sentiments of an old Alaskan sourdough.
I am one, but a revolution of kindness
is a vision of social justice.

It is about gender sensitive tough love
that accepts people of all nations
and all sexual persuasions
as precious children of God
with talents to share in ministry.
It is a call for renewal
and a search for the meaning of life.

Kindness is the key that opens
locked doors of a broken heart
and offers the gift of precious life.
Kindness saves lives.

I cannot relieve all the world's suffering,
but my poetry is an attempt to gently scatter flowers
upon the wind, wafting sweet aroma
to be enjoyed by one and all.

Kindness is the language
known around the world.
I cannot give all the kindness the world needs,
but the world needs all the kindness I can give.

(These poems make some bold claims. See Appendix for Jesus' words for kindness and their significance in our global age that is so torn and threatened by violence. Also see my books, *A Relational Hermeneutic of Kindness* and *A Relational Trinity of Kindness,* for why I make Kindness the prism for understanding God, the Bible, and our relationship to all people, indeed, to all things. Please read these poems as my humble prayer for healing and a desire to recapture truth, beauty, goodness, and zest in our lives).

Part One: Kindness is Relational

A philosophy of kindness comes naturally
when you understand that we live in a relational world.
—Kat Rose

"There's nothing weak about kindness and compassion.
There's nothing weak about
looking out for others.
There's nothing weak about being honorable."
—Barack Obama, spoken at funeral
for Elijah Cummings

Daybreak Solace

Come sunrise
warm my face
with your caressing rays.

See me start my day in kindness
to keep some souls from aching
and some hearts from breaking.

Spirit of Kindness

"Kindness and peace to you from
the one who was, who is,
and who is to come." (Author's translation of Revelation 1:4).

"God said, I am who I am.
I will show merciful kindness
on whom I wish." (Exodus 33:19).

What is the meaning of these Scriptures
for history of God relating to humans
in all ages and ages to come?

God's covenantal relationship to Israel,
God incarnate in Jesus,
and God's presence in world religions
is the biography of God.

How will this biography end?
Is there hope that good
will triumph over evil?

The 13 billion years of evolutionary history says yes.
The triumph of resurrection of Jesus over cross says yes.
Survival of world religions motivated by kindness says yes!
Meaning of life says yes.
Presence of saints like Mother Teresa says yes.

Despite the pessimistic attitude
pervading our culture today,
I basically remain an optimist.

Dictators rise and fall.
They always fall.
Hold onto that historical fact,
while working for a spirit of kindness
and justice for all persons.

Heart Seeds of Love

In the spirit of Saint Francis,
I serve sunflower heart seeds daily
on my deck communion rail.

My friends come acrobatically
flipping and dipping in excitement.
All are welcomed in kindness.

Even the bully boastful magpies
who send the small birds into hiding,
are received with loving heart gifts.

What God likes best
is showing kindness,
justice, and mercy
to everyone on earth.
(Jeremiah 9:24).

D. Cole

Always be gentle and love each other—Based on Galatians 4:32

Gentle love is the sunshine
in which flowers grow.
"Kindness is
the language which the
deaf can hear
and the blind can see."
—Mark Twain

Kindness is All Inclusive

I have been accused
of reducing the Bible to one theme---
the message of kindness.

I confess,
I am guilty as charged.
I have kindness intoxication.

I was nurtured in kindness
by my parents and grandparents,
my extended family
and faith family.

In my study and church ministry,
I was nurtured in kindness
by professors, deacons, elders,
and saintly church members.

In these reciprocal loving relationships
kindness flowered,
offering the balm of healing
perfume, sweet smelling incense.

Does this mean everyone
was always kind?

No, sometimes we all are unkind.
Unkind actions
are part of every person's life story
and of the Bible's story.

Yet, when I take the pulse of the Bible,
indeed, the pulse of the universe,
I find that Kindness is the heartbeat—

Kindness that is partial in us
is all-embracing in God.

Part II

My theology and creed is this:
God meets each moment of
our lives with kindness,
and calls us to be kind to others.

Our theology and creeds express
the heartbeat of our living faith
found in the Bible stories
and practiced in communal living.

The Bible itself was written
over a 1,000 year period
from stories told and retold
before being written down.

These stories were shaped
by the culture in which
they were told and written down.

It is helpful when we read the Bible today
to ask two questions:
What did the story mean when it was written?
What does the story mean today?

These two questions are the structure
of my hermeneutic of kindness.

(For more on the shaping of the Bible's story and why we should highlight kindness, see my books: *The Story of the Bible: Authority, Inspiration, Canonization, and Translation, A Relational Hermeneutic of Kindness, A Relational Trinity of Kindness. Gentle Galilean Glories: The Tender Teachings of Jesus*).

Kindness Blessing

May kindness be in our thoughts,
making them good and loving.
May kindness be in our eyes,
leading us to see what is just in life.

May kindness be in our hands and feet
so that we may be of service to others.
May kindness be in our whole being –

Making us one with God,
one with all people,
and one with the universe.

I don't know how to define kindness,
but I know for sure when I feel it.

Kindness is the language
known around the world.

Some have objected—
But kindness is simply
not in a lot of the Bible!

I would readily admit this.
War and vengeance were big societal forces
that shaped the biblical stories.
All the more reason—

We need to gather
all the persons, words, and stories
that show kindness;
and use them as a prism for reading the whole Bible
and all of our life experiences.

Kindness is a beautiful
stain glass window
that gathers the light of heaven
and warms all in its glow.

Practice Kindness

What do we live for,
if it is not to make life
less difficult for each other?
               —George Eliot

Tell me, pastor.
What is your day like?

I practice kindness.

If you learn of tragedy and death,
how do you respond?

I practice kindness.

When others want to build walls,
What do you say?

I practice kindness.

When nature is abused,
How do you respond?

I practice kindness.

If you go on vacation,
how do you act?

I practice kindness.

God has spoken:
Be kind to my children!

Based on Isaiah 40:1-2   D. Cole

"Kindness is the sunshine
in which virtue grows."
—Robert Ingersoll

Haiku Challenges

Truly God has said
Be kind to all my children
The world is waiting

Child taken from parents
held in cage like animals
Angels weep sad tears

To enter heaven
become as a little child
All nature mourns

Yes, God has spoken
Be kind to my little ones
Heaven is waiting

Kindness the sunshine
In which virtues are nurtured
Hope is created

Part Two: Kindness Is Healing

Kindness heals the head
and the heart

Free from Terror

Today I feel the ebb and flow of life.
Watching acrobatic redpolls.
Gazing at beautiful mountains—

Dorian pounds with vengeance.
Gun violence fills the airways.
Rocked in the cradle of terror—

Will I be a victim of violence?
Will our children go to school
to hear bells ring Bang! Bang!

Never to come home again.

In fear I crawled up the mountain.
Rocked in the cradle of terror—
The deep deep fearful abyss.

I still carry in my genes,
memories rocked in the cradle.
Nurtured in tender ways.

Memories roll from my eyes.
Trickled down my cheeks.
Memories of my caring family.

Rocked in the cradle of love.
I sit and listen to bird songs.
Hear lullabies of God's care for me.

Rocked in the cradle of kindness.

I join the chorus.
Step out of my body.
Break into blossom.

Rocked in the cradle of kindness.

Loving kindness casts out fears.
Restores broken hearts.
Kindness wins the day.

Kindness Rainbow

God's rainbow promises
are expressions of kindness
that heal head stress and heart strain.

My Big Idea—

My big idea is kindness.
If I had a bullhorn
I would sound kindness
from the mountain tops of Denali, Alaska
to the tip of Florida's most Southern shore.

Kindness among
all my brothers and sisters,
at home and beyond our borders
every one has value.

What is your big idea?
In America we can do anything!
Especially, learn to be Kind!
Right!!!

Go gently into nature
and find that it is good
and restores the soul.
D. Cole

Poetry of kindness
Washes travel stains of life
Restoring the soul

D. Cole

Garden Magic

When the world falls apart
keep the memory of a spring garden
where every flower petal
is a little heart.

When the world falls apart
flowers will still be giving.
The birds will still be singing.
Bees will still be humming their part.

All playing a joyful Psalm.
Inviting us to open our soul
and let the symphony make us whole.
Nature is a praise song.

We must save our gardens
If everything falls down
the spirit will still fly in and out.
In the garden everything is music.

Tenderness is Everything

Some mornings
after reading the newspaper criers
and catching the chyron,
the news crawl across the bottom of the tv screen,
I feel ashamed at being a human.

The homeless refugees
are asked to stay at home (?)
How inhumane is this!
Take the torch from the hand of the Statue Lady.
Wipe her tears with her gown.
Remove her crown.

When my heart is breaking
and I can stand no more,
I go for a long walk into the foothills
of the Chugach mountain range.

I sit on a snowy knoll
and watch the alpenglow sunrise unfold.
Gazing at the eternal miracle
that no-one can ever ban,
I shed the darkness,
like removing one garment at a time.

The gift of nature,
the tremor of pure sunlight
overcoming exhaustion,
the luminous tender touch we cherish.
The glow of heaven we so need,
the multitudes to keep and feed.

Wing Songs

Alleluia,
Hands to heaven
Kindness, carry us
Along

Hold us close
Don't ever leave us
Be our wings
of eternal songs

Kindness, kindness
We adore thee
We have found
Our long-lost home

Breathe your Union
hold our family
Cherish our
Eternal Song

Union, union
Be our union
Bless it through
Your Sacred Spirit

Take my thanks
I bring it to thee
Kiss me, hold me
Make me whole.

Kindness Energy.

The church has not yet incorporated Einstein's physics
into its theology and creeds.
Einstein's equation $E=mc^2$
shows that everything is made of energy
and radiates energy.
The energy of loving kindness powered Jesus' ministry
In a time when fear ran rampant.
Jesus' gentle teachings demonstrated that love casts out fear.
Fear controls many today and is the cause of many illnesses.
Acts of loving kindness radiate healing energy.
Stale theology entombed in old credal statements loses this vital healing energy.
Loving kindness is like a spiritual medicine pouring healing energy
into our body and into our relationships.

For the last twenty-five years I have tried to let loving kindness
be the steps that move my ministry.
In one sense this has been a return to the energized beginning of my ministry.
As a youth I gave a speech entitled,
"Love my Motive for Soul Winning."

With this speech I entered the youth speaker's tournament
in my home church and won.
I then gave it in the local Association of churches, winning again.
I next won the regional competition
and went to the State competition where I placed third.
By this time the theme of love was securely embedded in my soul.

The books I have published have pulled together my life's work
of sermons, prayers, and teaching material around
the hermeneutical theory of kindness
and draw on the insights of process philosophy. See my book,
The Apostle's Creed, for seeing how the creeds can be given
transforming energy when they are fleshed out with Jesus' gentle teachings
of loving kindness.

D. Cole

Gift of Kindness

Kindness, heart of God,
In your gentle fold,
We enter
All people become family
Where your kindness dwells.
God waits, the world waits.
Longing for this new family, Flesh and blood do not make us one. Union of love
and kindness Make us family.
Let us all taste the gift of kindness.
The fruit of God's own self.
The kiss of kindness, A healing balm
for all the world to share.

Part II

Go gently into nature
Receive its precious gifts,
Become one with all things.

I feel most alive contemplating,
experiencing first hand,
the union of my soul and nature's soul.

In this relationship kindness thrives
with each partner experiencing
the tenderness of the other.

Tenderness changes everything---
heals hurt and brings peace,
the union of oneness.

The gift of tenderness is experienced
as I watch a mother moose and new born calf
touch foreheads and dance.

The essence of the universe
is in that tender touch and love tango.

(I should have been taking video.
They were actually dancing around).

Flower Kisses

If you do not live in kindness
You will dwell where flowers wilt.
Flowers thrive by kissing
the soft rays of the morning sun
and gently sipping the dew drops.

Part II

flowers open reaching for the heavens
in each the sun and moon are hidden
each a star poem in which
God whispers love
and rests

Rose Haiku

roses thrive kissing
soft rays of the morning sun
sipping morning tea

Part Three: Kindness Is Justice

Concerning the proper treatment of foreigners,
Leviticus 19:34 commands:
"You shall love him as you love yourself,
for you my people were once strangers in the land of Egypt."
And regarding those most vulnerable in society,
Deuteronomy 24:17–18 instructs:
"Do not withhold justice from an outsider or an orphan,
and do not take the cloak of a widow in pledge.
Remember that you were slaves in Egypt
and that the LORD your God redeemed you from there.
Therefore, I am commanding you to do this."

Caravans of Hope

Be kind, for everyone you meet is fighting a hard battle.
                                        —Philo

Compassion for the weak is a sign of greatness.
                                        —Myles Munroe

Traversing miles
of oceans and lands.
Pushing and shoving
a great caravan.

Thousands of souls
desiring to be free.
A morning hymn—
Faces a Psalm to God.

God meets each event of life with kindness
and is always on the side of sojourners.
To oppose the wayfaring
strangers is to oppose God.

They are the face of God.
Tears of sadness
washing from the soul
the travel stains of life.

What shall our America
do with you home seekers?
Shall we lose the gifts
and skills you bring?

Come to new birth
On a new earth!
Faith, love,
and stout hearts.

Come caravans teeming.
Mother-care weary with child.

Father haunted by yesterday's sorrows
Hunted by new hope filled tomorrows.

Reach for the stars/stripes streaming.
Our America and yours dreaming.

Spark the flame of second birth.
Resurrection mirth.

The greatest gift we have is
the power of kindness. D. Cole

If eyes are made for seeing
then beauty needs no other reason
for being

(Based on "The Rhodora," Ralph Waldo Emerson)

Tenderness in Nature

Go into nature to dwell
on the tender elements in the world.

Experience the presence
of eternity in the beauty of nature.

Sense the immediacy of a kingdom
not of this world quietly revealing love

Flowers of the fields
Birds of the air.

All revealing
God's healing

that quietly comes
by love for you and me.

Kindness is Everything

There is an organic affinity
between joyousness and tenderness.
—William James

If you want to be happy.
Be kind to yourself.

If you want others to be happy.
Be kind to them.

If you want nature to be happy.
Be kind to birds, flowers, bees, and trees.

If you want to be happy
Be kind.

Song of Victory

Joyfully we seek you, God of kindness.

You are always blessing---

birds singing a sweet melody

the summer sun caressing the flowers.

Let us taste the gift of your kindness---

March together arm in arm

heart to heart.

Kindness is the language

Known and heard around the world.

Sing the song of victory—

Kindness to all.

The triumphant song of eternity.

The Meaning of Life

The purpose of life is to serve,
and to show compassion and the will to help others.
Albert Schweitzer

One of the most asked questions around the world—
What is life all about?
We especially ask,
What is the meaning of my suffering?

The questions are so many:
Why did my child die in a school shooting?
Why was my son killed in this terrible war?
Why was my family lost in a car accident?

Why?

As a minister I had to answer these questions.
From the slender threads of broken lives
I tried to weave patterns of meaning.
In asking why one can find a

How?

Here is the how:
All life is precious, has value,
and holds potential meaning
under any circumstance.

We can not always choose
what life deals to us,
but we can choose our reaction
to what is dealt.

Here is the path of how,
leading to healing:

Find someone to listen,
comfort, console.

Focus with that person
on the precious moments you still have.

Center on goodness, grace, and love.

If you can not find that person,
go gently into nature
and be still.

Nature will be kind to you.
Nature has healing
and restoring powers.

Kindness is as sweet as honey

Sipping Honey

The worker bees
are sipping honey
for this is what they do.
Free, free as the breeze.

Their labor lasts
only about five weeks.
But if one can fly from
flower to flower—

Nuzzling happiness,
hour by hour

All in
a Garden of Eden
with heaven's sunlight
shining over them.
that might be
enough sweetness.

Be Kind

As a linguist,
I have seen how words are powerful
and the precursor to action---
Hostile words often lead
to hostile actions.

Kindness is like honey—
Sweet to the taste
and healing to the soul.

Taste and see that God is
good,
loving,
and kind.

Be kind to one another.

I believe!

When the foundations
of our world order shake
I go out to consider the wild flowers.
Rocked in eternity's arms.

I seek the One
who envisions primordial aims,
daily lures beauty and goodness.
Rocked in eternity's arms.

Become one with the sun, moon,
and stars in orbit.
Shines in the sunshine and the rain.
Rocked in eternity's arms.

I sit and listen to bird songs
Hear lullabies
of God's care for me.
Rocked in the cradle of kindness.

I join the chorus.
Step out of my body
Break into blossom.
Rocked in the cradle of kindness.

Where kindness dwells,
God lives.
I believe!

Wings of Glory

Come little bird in flight
Soft as rose petals falling
Art book pages flipping

Wishing to know love's meaning
We commune with each other
Hope flutters from heart to heart

Heart felt choristers
Sing together as friends
A song of tenderness and love

Light of glory beamed
in this new friendship
O wondrous power of touch
sweet meaning it brings

Spirit of nature caressing
Soul beauty possessing
What can not be
But eternally is

Friendship with nature's beauty
Leads to tenderness for all in pain
Light from heaven does not shine in vain

Felt soul-quakes
Letting the glory in
My spirit took wing and flew

Tenderness is Everything

Walt Whitman gave us some wise advise
in the preface to *Leaves of Grass*—

Argue not concerning God.
Re-examine all you have been told
at church or school or in any book.
Dismiss whatever insults your soul.

We are living in troubling times.
Walls of hatred and exclusion
are being erected between cultures and nations.
We desperately need to be building bridges
between religions, cultures, and nations.

in dismissing what insults the soul,
we need a compass
for steering our lives in stormy times.

That compass is tenderness.

My basic philosophical belief
Is that all life is interconnected and interrelated.
Theologically, I believe
God is in all things giving value
and relating tenderly in saving ways,
luring us to become our best self.

Centering on the beauty and wonder
of relational tenderness found in most
cultures and religions
is the best route to peace in our global age.
Nurturing tenderness is also the route
to saving our environment and endangered planet.

(I did not just decide one day
to take this photo of nuthatch
eating from my hand.

I spent all summer gaining the trust
of my nuthatch friends
by daily filling the saucer
with heart seeds,
one kind act at a time.

Kindness is nurturing
and transforming.
This poem and its meaning,
keeps growing for me.
From Emily Dickinson I learned
that hope is a thing with feathers.
In William Wordsworth's most famous poem,
The Prelude (215 pages), I experienced
his deep love of nature, and how
this experience of tenderness leads to love
for all things, including love for all people.)

(These two nuthatch photos and poem, Wings of Glory, were taken from my book,
Wings of Inspiration)

True Friendship

I know a friendship that is true
Formed in the Chugach foothills
Where nature welcomes all

A contemplative feeds nuthatches
that visit his deck daily
in all kinds of weather

In spite of seasons
that come and go
Love never fails

Heart seeds extended in hand
Pecked one by one
Feathers caressed trembling

Faithful friendship formed
Hope sent through air
Love sings

Kindness is reciprocal
Hearts beat as one
Take wings and fly

In quiet contemplation I discover three great life changing
treasures —
Beauty, goodness, and kindness.

Wrapped in Kindness

After a day of showing tender care for my grandchildren
I was sitting in my rocking chair
enjoying the cool crisp air.

This mother to be moose
nibbled some tender twigs
just below my deck.
Then looking intently into my soul
she honored me by bedding down,
almost in my lap,
in the soft snow,
with her warm fur blanket
tucked snugly under her chin.
With my soul nurtured
I followed her trusting example
and went to bed wrapped
in faith and kindness.

Kindness Training Exercise

Poetry of Kindness is about relational kindness. Relational is key. Life is about relationships from birth till death. Relational kindness comes naturally in family and community, and flows in personal ways. Emphasizing the relational aspects of kindness broadens the definition, moving kindness beyond the emotional to include courageous acts of kindness issuing in justice.

Mindfully setting aside times to meditate on how we can better show kindness can help us become more sensitive and responsive to others within our everyday circles and move to include all persons.

Find a quiet time each day to prayerfully think about what you desire for your family and yourself:

* To be safe and secure
* To be happy and at peace
* To have good health
* To be free from fear
* To have fun times for all in family
* To be kind to each other and all people, animals, and all living things
* Showing kindness is a healing activity. Consciously think kind thoughts throughout your daily activity and feel those energies flowing to others in courageous actions.

With this kindness growing in your life, every day is a dream and every tomorrow a vision of hope.

Conclusion

Seeing With New Eyes

Little chickadee
lands so lightly in my hand
Looks into my eyes
I experience soul quakes
Heaven opens angels sing

I see with new eyes
all little birds of the world
Coming in such trust
I see every butterfly
every bee lighting on me

See every sunrise
Every cloud and drop of rain
All life giving gifts
Spinning universe in eyes
Mysteries from unseen realms

Birds visiting my deck
Come from many parts of world
Journey work of stars
Forever perishing
Yet living eternally

Transforming miracles
Compassion growing for all
Love for humankind
Hope in my hands and heart
Treat everyone with kindness

A Summary Vision of Kindness

Gentleness, self-sacrifice, and generosity
are the exclusive possession of no one race or religion.
Mahatma Gandhi

Kindness is the key for understanding
the loving and generous heart beat of nature.

My vision for the world is that we will learn
to be kind to each other.

The inner nourishing of a kind spirit in every person
Is one of the most important needs in our world today.

Kindness in one's heart
is felt by the universe.

Yet, I am painfully aware of the chasm between this vision
and its ultimate expression in our world that is so divided.

People of all faith persuasions are called
to refocus on tender teachings that see value in all persons.

Visions may be expressed in gentle words,
but they are more powerful when expressed in tender actions.

The kindness one shows to family and others
is the most healing force in the world.

Centered in kindness
We can transform our world.

Will you join me in thinking kind thoughts—
Kindness Is Every Step?

Gift of Kindness

Kindness is our best gift
to a complicated and cruel world.

we cannot show all the kindness
the world needs,

but the world needs
all the kindness we can give.

Appendix A
JESUS' WORDS OF GENTLENESS AND KINDNESS
Πραυς, Πραυτης (gentle, gentleness)

In reference to persons, πραυς and πραυτης, the noun and adjective form, are best translated as gentle and gentleness. The two terms are used about 15 times in the Greek New Testament and may also be translated as meek, humble, friendly, or pleasant, in both adjective and noun forms.

In the Old Testament gentleness is rooted in God. The inheritance of the land promised to Abraham and his descendants comes to the gentle who wait---"The humble will possess the land and enjoy prosperity and peace" (See Psalms 37:9-11).

In the New Testament, the mission of Jesus is the fulfillment of gentleness. In fact, it is the self-designation of Jesus in Matthew 11:28-30--"Come to me, all of you who are tired from carrying heavy loads, and I will give you rest. Take my yoke and put it on you, and learn from me, because I am gentle and humble in spirit; and you will find rest. For the yoke I will give you is easy and the load I will put on you is light."

That Jesus was πραυς, tender of heart, is also supported by the Letters of Paul in the New Testament and in non-biblical sources like the Gospel of Thomas, the Sibylline Oracles, and Pistis Sophia. In Second Corinthians chapter ten, verse one, Paul wrote, "Jesus himself was humble and gentle." Colossians 3:12 grounds kindness in the being of God, "You are God's people so be gentle, kind, humble, and meek." Titus 3:4 also describes God as kind.

ταπεινος, ταπεινοω, ταπεινωσις

This group of Greek words occurs thirty-four times in the New Testament, and they are usually translated "lowly", but they carry the connotation of gentle or gentleness..

χρηστος

Jesus used χρηστος twice, once to describe the nature of God as kind to the ungrateful and wicked (Luke 6:35) and once as a self-designation, describing himself as one who is kind or merciful in what he requires of those who come to him (Matthew 11:30).

Paul understood kindness in this way as well. In Romans 2:4 he writes about the "fullness of the χρηστητος, kindness, of God and God's patience, μακροθυμιας. In Romans 11:22 Paul speaks of the kindness of God being shown for the ones who have fallen away from God. In these uses of kindness Paul is true to the Old Testament understanding of the gracious action of God and he sees this fulfilled in the actions of Jesus. In Galatians 5:22-23 Paul listed kindness as one of the fruits of the Spirit that should be growing in the life of Christians.

1 Peter 2:2-3, shows the saving action of kindness. "Like new born infants, long for the pure spiritual milk , so that by it you may grow into salvation. If indeed you have tasted that the Lord is good and kind, χρηστος.

The crowning verse on kindness in the New Testament for Christians is Ephesians 4:32---"Be kind and merciful, and forgive others, just as God forgave you because of Christ." This key verse links kindness with forgiveness and anchors these qualities in God's own actions with the gentle ministry of Jesus.

ελεος

Ελεος occurs three times in Matthew and is usually translated as mercy. The Good News Bible translates it as kindness, its original Old Testament meaning. This can be seen in Matthew 9:9-11, which reports Jesus' call of Matthew to discipleship. After Jesus called Matthew, he was having a meal in Matthew's house with other tax collectors and outcasts. Some Pharisees saw this and asked Jesus' disciples, "Why does Jesus eat with such people?" Jesus heard them and answered, "People who are well do not need a doctor, but only those who are sick. Go and find out what is meant by the scripture that says, 'It is kindness that I want, not animal sacrifices.' I have not come to call respectable people, but outcasts." This and the other two passages in Matthew that use ελεος (12:7; 23:23) characterize Jesus' ministry as merciful kindness toward the outcasts and demand the same for the disciples who would follow Jesus.

Ελεος, mercy, occurs six times in Luke. Five of these are in the birth announcements of John and Jesus and refer to the wonderful kindness and tender mercy God is showing toward the people of God (Luke 1:50, 54, 58, 72, 78). Tender mercy is most relevant to the theme of "Gentle Galilean Glories:" "Our God is merciful and tender. God will cause the bright dawn of salvation to rise on us and to shine from heaven on all those who live in the dark shadow of death, to guide our path to peace."

σπλαγχνον, σπλανγχνιζομαι

In Luke 1:78, ελεος is combined with σπλαγχνον and is translated as "tender mercy." The verb form, σπλαγχνιζομαι, occurs twelve times in Matthew, Mark, and Luke, the Synoptic Gospels, and is usually translated as "having compassion." Ten of these represent Jesus as one in whom divine compassion is present. Jesus is moved with compassion toward a man with a dreaded skin disease (Mark 1:41). the crowd of people who were like sheep without a shepherd (Mark 6:34; Matthew 14:14), and the hungry crowd (Mark 8:2: Matthew 15:32).

Jesus also had compassion on the widow of Nain and raised her dead son back to life (Luke 7:11-17), and with compassion he restored sight to two blind men (Matthew 20:29-34). The verb, having compassion, also had a central place in three of Jesus' most significant parables: the unforgiving servant who had been forgiven with compassion (Matthew 18:21-33), the good Samaritan whose heart was filled with compassion when he saw the wounded man lying by the roadside (Luke 10:25-37. The whole Samaritan story is summarized as an act of kindness. and the parable of the prodigal son, better called the waiting father, for it is the father who saw the son a long way off and had compassion and ran to meet him (Luke 15:11-32, especially see verse 20).

In all of these teachings of Jesus that use σπλαγχνον and σπλαγχνιζομαι, Jesus' human emotions are described in the strongest terms possible in order to stress the tender compassion with which God claims persons in saving grace. This was also true of all the other Greek words we have studied.

χαρις

The χαρις word group appears about 175 times in the New Testament, with the majority occurring in the Epistles of Paul. Most English versions of the Bible translate χαρις as grace or gracious. However, the *Contemporary English Version* of the American Bible Society almost always translates χαρις as kindness. A survey of the history of the term from its early Greek origins to the time of the New Testament justifies this use of kindness. In both the Old Testament and the New Testament the Hebrew and Greek words usually translated as grace imply a kind turning of one person to another in an act of assistance. God's covenant grace also implies kindness.

Perhaps the most significant uses of χαρις come in the Book of Revelation. At a time when the followers of Jesus are being persecuted and dying for their faith, John the writer of Revelation holds up a vision of the kind Jesus. The book starts with this prayer: "I pray that you will be blessed with kindness and peace from God, who is and was and is coming. May you receive kindness and peace from Jesus, the faithful witness" (Based on Revelation 1:4-5 from the SEP

Greek New Testament). Revelation ends with this prayer: "I pray that Jesus will come soon and be kind to all of you" (Based on Revelation 22:20-21 from the Greek New Testament. For a fuller treatment of this Greek word see my book, *The Book of Revelation: Jesus' Kindness Transforms Suffering*).

The word clusters we have examined leave no room for doubt that Jesus was gentle, lowly, and kind.. What struck me as I studied Jesus' language of kindness was how Jesus described himself as being gentle. Thus, we are on solid ground when we speak of Jesus as kindness. The kindness of God shines in the words and deeds of Jesus. The disciples and the crowds who followed Jesus saw the glory of God shining through his gentle Galilean glories. Can there be any doubt that Jesus lived and taught kindness? The rich cluster of words described above make kindness a good choice for our relational hermeneutic of kindness.

Appendix B
JESUS IS KIND: Ten Key Biblical Verses

1. "God's love and **kindness** will shine upon us like the sun that rises in the sky. On us who live in the dark shadow of death, this light will shine to guide us into a life of peace" (Luke 1:78-79).

2. Jesus said, "Come to me, all of you who are tired from carrying heavy loads, and I will give you rest. Take my yoke and put it on you, and learn from me, because I am **gentle and humble in spirit**; and you will find rest. For the yoke I will give you is easy and the load I will put on you is light." (Matthew 11:28-30).

3. Jesus said, "**Blessed are the gentle**, they will receive what God has promised!" (Matthew 5:5).

4. Paul in imitating the spirit of Jesus, grounds kindness in the being of God, "You are God's people so **be gentle, kind, humble, and meek**." (Colossians 3:12).

5. "**Be kind and merciful**, and forgive others, just as God forgave you because of Jesus." (Ephesians 4:32).

6. Jesus taught, "People who are well do not need a doctor, but only those who are sick. Go and find out what is meant by the scripture that says, 'It is **kindness** that I want, not animal sacrifices.' I have not come to call respectable people, but outcasts." (Matthew 9:12-13).

7. "I pray that you will **be blessed with kindness** and peace from God, who is and was and is coming. May you receive kindness and peace from Jesus, the faithful witness." (Revelation 1:4-5).

8. "A man with leprosy came to Jesus and knelt down. **Jesus felt sorry for him** so he put his hands on him and said, 'You are well.'" (Mark 1:40-41).

9. "Jesus said, "Don't worry about your life. **God will take care of you**." (Luke 12:22-26).

10. "I pray that **Jesus will be kind to all of you**." (Revelation 22:21).

Appendix C
Importance of Gentle Teachings

Gentle teachings ring true in all cultures and can be a unifying theme for dialogue between most religions of the world, offering a path to peace. Following the amazing discoveries of the genome project, the mapping of the human chromosomes, biologists speak of the genetic unity of all living things, believing that all organisms descended from the same ancestral life forms. Thus far the genome project has shown that the common ancestor of all living things was similar to single-celled microbes with the simplest molecular composition that go back several billion years. Thus all living things share a molecular history and are interrelated, interconnected.

This dialogue must take place if we are to have reconciliation between the world religions and find a route to peace. The greatest challenge to theistic religions is the pervasive reality of evil and the misery it leaves in its wake. This unifying theme of gentleness is one possible solution to this problem, especially the growing divide between Christianity and Islam.

"Loving-kindness" is a major theme in Judaism. The Psalms of the Old Testament are full of this concept that is key to understanding God and God's people. Since Judaism gave birth to Christianity and Islam, the two largest religions in the world, this unifying theme is something all three religions hold in common. "Metta" is a strong concept in Buddhism and carries the meaning of loving kindness or unconditional love. Buddha said, "My religion is kindness." He sought love without attachment. In much Buddhist thought love when practiced moves from self to friend, to enemy, and to all beings everywhere. "Karuna" or compassion that leads one to assist others is also key. Meaningful dialogue could be held around the theme of gentle teachings that could transform the relationships of these major religions.

Also, the longer I have lived with the New Testament the more I have become convinced that a major thrust of these sacred scriptures is to show the humanity of Jesus. We have focused on this purpose without violating any natural biological processes, and this makes Jesus' sacrificial death on the cross more meaningful with more transforming power. This approach also opens the door to see that other major religious leaders like Moses, Confucius, Mohammed, Buddha, Gandhi, and Martin Luther King, Jr. can also self-actualize creative love aims and purposes that transform lives and our world.

One may not be able to write a biographical account of the life of Jesus. My graduate study in New Testament led me on a search for the historical Jesus and I read all the major sources and many lives of Jesus, some in French and German. I have tried to keep up with the new search for the historical Jesus and the Jesus seminars. However, I do believe you can locate in the Gospels the authentic gentle teachings of Jesus. Whether they all come from Jesus, some come from the Gospel writers, or some from the early Church community, really do not matter in one sense. They are all inspired by Jesus gentle ministry and remain insightful, challenging teachings that can change and transform lives and offer a path to peace.

Jesus' Galilean vision of reality has flickered through many cultures since the time of Jesus, but it has never been fully realized. Yet Jesus' vision still holds the promise of creative advance and world transformation. (For more on Jesus' gentle Teachings see my book, *Gentle Galilean Glories: The Tender Teachings of Jesus*).

Appendix D
GOD IS KIND

Ten Key Bible Verses Based on Contemporary English Version

1. "I am God, and I am merciful and **kind**" (Based on Exodus 33:19).

2. "God blesses those who live right, and shields them with **kindness**" (Psalm 5:12).

3. "God, you brought me safely through birth, and you protected me as a baby at my mother's breast. From the day I was born I have been in your **tender care**, and from my birth you have been by my side." (Psalm 22:9-10).

4. "There are some who ask, 'Who will be good to us?' Let your **kindness**, God, shine brightly on us. You brought me more happiness than a rich harvest of grain and grapes. I can lie down and sleep soundly because you will keep me safe." (Psalm 4:6-8).

5. "God's **kindness** and love will always be with me each day of my life, and I will live forever in God's house." (Psalm 23:6).

6. "Please God, be **kind** to us!" (Isaiah 33:2).

7. "Our God has said, encourage my people! Give them comfort. **Speak kindly** to Jerusalem and announce good news." (Isaiah 40:1-2).

8. "Just as shepherds care for their flocks, God will carry you in arms of compassion and **gently** lead you." (Isaiah 40:11).

9. "I have learned to **feel safe** and satisfied, just like a child on its mother's lap. People of God, you must trust God now and forever." (Psalm 131).

10. "I pray that you will be blessed with **kindness** from God." (Revelation 1:4.

(Since all my writing and poems are influenced by process philosophy, I am including these key quotes from Whitehead's writings on tenderness that shape my understanding of God).

Alfred North Whitehead on Kindness

Whitehead often wrote of the **tender** element in the teachings of Jesus as expressing the essence of Christianity and having persuasive influence:

"There can be no doubt as to what elements in the record have evoked a response from all that is best in human nature. The Mother, the Child, and the bare manger: the lowly man, homeless and self-forgetful, with his message of peace, love, and sympathy: the suffering, the agony, the **tender** words as life ebbed, the final despair: and the whole with the authority of supreme victory."

Whitehead thought that philosophical theology should provide "a rational understanding of the rise of civilization and the **tenderness** of mere life itself."

"Whitehead held the Galilean origin of Christianity in high regard:

It dwells upon the **tender** elements in the world, which slowly and in quietness operate by love; and it finds purpose in the present immediacy of a kingdom not of this world."

In speaking of the wisdom of God's subjective aim, Whitehead writes: "The image---and it is but an image---the image under which this operative growth of God's nature is best conceived, is that of a **tender** care that nothing be lost."

In speaking of the consequent nature of God, Whitehead says that God saves the world as it passes into the immediacy of God's own life. "It is the judgment of a **tenderness** which loses nothing that can be saved."

In the same vein he writes that God does not create the world; God saves the world. God is the poet of the world, "with **tender** patience leading it by his vision of truth, beauty, and goodness." (Whiteheads's reference to Galilean origins of Christianity inspired my book, *Gentle Galilean Glories: The Tender Teachings of Jesus*).

Other Writings on Kindness by Dwayne Cole

(My book, *A Relational Trinity of Kindness*, is a fresh interpretation of the Trinity through the prism of kindness)

A Relational Trinity of Kindness

A Relational Trinity of Kindness
is a door that is never locked

Opening the door reveals our great companion
Who understands and suffers with us

Open the door
Find healing mercy

Transforming our actions
into heaven's reality

Perishing
Yet living forever

Poetry of Kindness and Trinity

I once represented the power of the cathedral,
wearing my ministerial robe and seasonal stoles.

As a sermon writer turned poet,
I affirm the power of the individual.

In my nature poetry I wrap divine images
with my personal visionary dreams.

In this matrix the power of poetry is born,
nurturing cultural aspirations.

Moses and the Old Testament prophets,
Confucius and the Buddha,

Mary and Saint Theresa,
and the tender teachings of Jesus,

all are one
in a poetry of kindness.

The transformative power of a poetry of kindness
negates the violent world

creating a vision
of beauty, goodness, and love.

This creative power of nature poetry
wrapped in tender teachings

is the hope
of our global age.

Poetry has the ability to join
science and the humanities,

religion and politics
in transforming the world.

Kindness as the name given to God,
Jesus, and Spirit

is to be understood
as the power of transformation.

The creative transforming powers of poetry
evoke mysterious images of beauty

that are difficult to capture
in other forms of prose media.

Adventures in Kindness

These latest eight books,
selected from the nineteen
I have published so far,
tell my adventure of ideas,
my vision of beauty,
goodness, and kindness,
largely in poetic format.

World Kindness Day

World Kindness Day, November 13, was launched by like minded organizations in 1998. The goal is to make the world a better place by celebrating and promoting good deeds of kindness. There are currently 28 nations involved in World Kindness Day which is not affiliated with any religion or political movement.

World Kindness Day, seeks to bind all people as one and bridge the divides between race, religion, politics, and gender. World Kindness Day was introduced in 1998 by the World Kindness Movement as a coalition of nations seeking a more kind and just world. This book of nature photos and poems seeks to make a contribution to world transforming kindness.

Those who know me and read my books and posts on Facebook, know that kindness is one of my major concerns. When I retired and moved to Alaska to help care for our grandchildren in 2011, I began to pull together the sermons I preached and the material I taught in college and seminary approved classes for fifty years. I found that the theme of kindness emerged as a dominant theme. In the eighteen previous books I have published, kindness is the hermeneutic, the prism, through which I understand God, the Bible, and the world. Each step of kindness contributes to inner peace and world peace.

My understanding of God can best be seen in my book, *A Relational Trinity of Kindness*. This transformative image of relational kindness is the heart of my book, *A Center that Holds: Adventures in Kindness*. Kindness as a hermeneutic for interpreting the Bible can best be seen in my world vision that unfolds in, *The Book of Revelation: Jesus' Kindness Transforms Suffering*. *(All ten of my books can be seen on Amazon.com*

I can not give all the kindness the world needs, but the world needs all the kindness I can give. The poem I wrote below for World Kindness Day expresses my prayerful gift:

Gift of Kindness

Joyfully we seek you, God of kindness.
You are always blessing—
birds singing a sweet melody,
flowers caressing the summer sun.

Let us taste the gift of your kindness—
March together arm in arm
heart to heart.

Kindness is the language
Known and heard around the world.

Sing the song of victory,
Kindness Is Every Step—
The triumphant song of eternity

CPSIA information can be obtained
at www.ICGtesting.com
Printed in the USA
BVHW021917200721
612427BV00001B/1